A Long Walk

A Father & Son's Words & Images

Tim Bienkowski and Andrew Bienkowski

POETRY:
Andrew Bienkowski
Tim Bienkowski
Family Members*

PHOTOGRAPHY:
Tim Bienkowski

EDITOR:
Tim Bienkowski

ACKNOWLEDGMENTS

Thanks to my father, Andrew, for imparting much wisdom to me over the years.

For Encouragement & Inspiration
_____

Rosemary Kothe
E.R. Baxter
Mary Akers
Ken Feltges

For Love & Support
_____

Toni Bienkowski
Zoe Kothe
Randy Bienkowski
Helen Schmidt
William Kothe

Thank you for allowing me to include additional poems from
_____

* Zoe Kothe
* Randy Bienkowski
* Helen Schmidt

CONTENTS

PREFACE

Poetry has been a great joy to my father and me. We both consider it to be the purist form of writing. My father likes to call it "the language of the soul." We write to figure things out for ourselves, and when the poems reveal something, we share them with each other and our loved ones.

Putting this collection together, I recognize the similarities in our poetry and views on life. As you read this collection, you may want to avoid looking at the author until you reach the bottom of the page. Hopefully the photography adds to the depth of the poetry. We hope you enjoy it!

Tim Bienkowski

1 NATURE

Island Of Peace

Enter my island of peace.
Travel the winding hilly roads
To my sanctuary.

Walk across my secure trusting bridge.
Take in the sound of the water.
Check your worries with the minnows
And listen to the stream's lullaby.

My creatures welcome you.
Songbirds continue their concert.
Small animals carry on their normal dance.

Pass the flowerbeds that surround me.
Let my scents intoxicate you
And my blooms raise your vibrations (of love).
They have been waiting for you.

Walk my grounds of fresh cut grass.
Its aroma reminding you of the rewards of
Weekly rituals of sweat and care.

My trees reach out to you,
Beeches and Elm shading you
From my brightest light.
A giant Pine watching over you
Constantly.

Enter my garden of abundance.
Diverse species of the exotic and ordinary.
A mysterious bed of ingredients for
Soups of endless possibilities and nourishment.

Lay in my steamy hot springs.
My heat melting away your worries.
Our energies exchanging through the mist.
Memory banks of details and structure
Giving way to imagination and newfound simplicity.

My caretakers have been expecting you.
They keep my windows shined,
Allowing my wisdom to be clearly received.

They live in harmony with my world,
And invite you to join them.
Listen to my voice in the silence,
And take my peace with you.
My island lies inside of you.

Tim Bienkowski

Walking On Your Mother's Back

She has provided you with a home
Fed you with the crops she grew
Caressed you with warm and gentle breezes
Surrounded you with nature's beauty
And taught you her ancient wisdom
Yes, mother Earth has been good to you
She loves you and protects you.

So, walk gently
On your mother's back.
Step softly on her ancient body.
Let each step
Be a kiss of gratitude and love.
Be kind to your mother.
She has been good to you.

When surrounded by the trees of her arms
Sit quietly, empty your mind,
And listen to her whispers
In the breeze.
Maybe if you are lucky
You will hear
Some of her ancient wisdom.

She has much to say about
Love, eternity, the universe, truth and beauty.

Andrew Bienkowski

Sand

Along the seashore I saunter,
Feet sinking in deep golden sand,
Slowing my steps at last,
Making me breathe deeper,
Sloughing the dead skin
From my soles,
Revitalizing my sense of balance,
I make a good impression
In the sand.

Tim Bienkowski

September Morning On Nauset Beach

6 a.m.
Brilliant sky suggests that the sun
will emerge from the ocean soon.
Full moon bright behind the dunes.
Wide expanse of sand for a mile
to the left and right is smooth
and clean, with only one set of footprints,
mine.

Colors from the sky bounce
on gentle waves. In the water
no more than 40 feet away
is a seal.
We watch each other intently.
I feel curiosity, amusement,
friendship, affection. I begin
to sing. First softly. The wordless tune
becomes a bridge between us.

As my chant becomes louder
the seal moves closer,
fascinated with the sound.
I sing my heart out. No need for words
the ancient melody flows,
connects us, reminds us
that we are part of the same
universe, same nature,
that on a deeper level
we are one.

The moment does not last.
The sun pops out of the ocean
ending the magic.
The song is silent,
the seal dives and disappears.
But this moment remains
etched deep
in my soul.

Andrew Bienkowski

Coming Home

She knelt thoughtfully next to the stream,
Listening to the constant song of the crickets,
The occasional flopping splashes of the bullfrogs,
And the gurgling murmur of the current.

Fireflies lit ever so briefly,
Like tiny flashbulbs recording the magic of the evening,
The film of her mind rewinding to a simpler time.

A little girl full of questions and dreams,
Escaping the world of expectations and rules.
Her toes now submerged in the spongy moss of the stream bed.
The unwavering music of the current overwhelming her with peace.

She never understood the power of the water,
But it made her feel complete.
Her worries drifting far downstream.

She heard her grandmother's words rise from the water.
That nature would take care of things.
That it always had.

She had forgotten essential truths.
To know our beds are bounded only by ourselves,
To listen to our own stream of consciousness,
To recognize what's simple is true.

She dipped her hands into the water,
Splashed her face with palms full,
And opened her eyes to awaken once more.

Tim Bienkowski

Nature Calling

Today's mysterious silence is nature's eternal symphony.
I hear the universe's song in every single raindrop.

Silence crashes like a wave upon my bustling soul,
Seeps in to quell this ancient desire.
No people here, just the breath of trees.
Fingerprints of nature to fill all eternity.

I want to break free of the chains on myself,
Chains of my mind and body.
I want to slip free out of my shell
And dissolve into the air,
Free forever.

The forest floor is a picture I will paint someday.
A picture that will tell of my soul.
Color and texture poured on paper,
When I am ready to speak of myself.
When you are ready to see and hear,
You will find me there.

Zoe Kothe

In Silence

My soul is greater than the sum of my parts.

Earth, water, fire and air flow thru my being.

Many have come to surround me by the stream.

Their love overwhelms me.

I ask them to stay awhile, to walk with me,

To wander and dream till the light fades.

Once before many years ago they came to

Wed and bless us.

Today in silence I know they have been here

All along.

I see their forms rising in the smoke,

And wonder who will tend the fire

When we are gone from here.

Helen Schmidt

2 BACKPACKING

The Journey

We march through this trail,
The weight of our worlds on our shoulders.
For how can we be without…
A roof over our heads,
Something to keep us warm at night,
Food to nourish us,
Familiar connections to our normal world.

But as we trudge through the mud,
And struggle for balance on the rocks,
We ponder…
Security weighs more than we thought.
Perhaps next time we will travel lighter.

Our steps will be springier,
Our footing surer,
Our eyes freer to wander,
Our spirit freer to soar.

The lightness of being requires only us.

Tim Bienkowski

Johnnycake Trail (Aug 05)

4 miles with 40 lbs. on your back to get there

2 days to connect to earth again

3 days to let go of the world left behind

4th day morning, 6 AM.
      I am the only human
      awake within 4 mile radius.

          Misty dawn,
          mysterious mountains,
          trees in a moist haze,
          mirror-like lake
          reflects the gray
          pre-sunrise sky.

It's calm and silent
the stillness echoes
in the stillness of the mind.
      Being here finally,
      just being
      not doing.

Calm, still, silent,
like the trees and the lake.

Being here in this moment,
It does not get better than this.

Andrew Bienkowski

Reentry

Driving back at 55 miles per hour
In this contraption of steel and rubber,
It hits me like a ton of bricks.
I am leaving the natural world,
Returning to one of technology,
To do lists, agendas,
And complications.

I want to go back…

Back to the porcupines,
The monarchs,
The high grass,
The fireflies,
The intensity of the sun,
The whisper of the wind,
The unraveling of the trail,
The voices of the forest,
Voices I must hear again.

Tim Bienkowski

3 LOVE

For Helen

This moment is special,
Worth holding on to.
I am lying down in a tent
Late at night
In the middle of a forest,
Miles from the nearest road.
It's quiet, I am comfortable
This peaceful moment
Is interrupted by a sudden
Violent rain, wind, lightning
And thunder.
I feel safe here in this dry tent,
Away from all the tools of civilization,
Electricity, phone, TV, radio, cars.
Human kind is not in charge here.
Mother nature rules.
In the daytime I see how
She expresses herself.
In the trees and flowers and ferns.
I feel love in her expressions.

And then when I think of love
I think of you.
I see love in your smiling face
And gentle eyes.
I think of you and I become
A gentler, kinder, warmer me.

I feel your love
The way I feel
The sun on my skin.
The soft touch of the sun
Is like the touch of your hand
That calms my soul
And tells me about love.

Here in the wilderness,
In the middle of a thunderstorm
I remember how you came into my life
And gave it meaning.

You don't know that
Without you in my life
I could not do
What I do.
I wouldn't want to,
I wouldn't care.

I would become a silent hermit,
Living away from people,
In a world of thought.

I look forward to seeing your smile
And hearing your laughter
That will make my heart sing.

Do you know that you are my Hafiz poem?

Written for Helen
On 8/8/03

Andrew Bienkowski

Zoe

She's a purple zebra,
Hopping through Paris,
Splashing through the desert
In her Ovaltine convertible.

She's sunshine slipping through
A cheeseburger surprise.
A dog-eared magazine
Who growls nicely.

She's a creamy Cannoli,
Taking shade beneath the bonsai's.
A violin concerto,
In search of worthy hands.

Tim Bienkowski

A Healing

He said "I love you",

And gently touched
The burning flesh.
Time stopped,
Darkness moved away
Into the shadows
Energy flowed through
The fingers.

Rearranging the atoms
And the molecules
Reconnecting broken synapses,
It felt like a cool
Waterfall,
Infused with bright rainbows
And tickling minnows.
She opened her eyes
And smiled
For the first time
In days.

Andrew Bienkowski

Shadows

Ancient shadows pull us together,
Memories etched into stone,
Reasons hidden within the earth.

You are my shadow lover,
Covering my imperfections
With your gentle ways.

The sun is bright
And we are alive,
Let's give these rocks
A moment to remember.

Tim Bienkowski

The Chalice

You are a chalice
Improved and Polished
By All that flows through.

Experience of pain and beauty,
Discipline and courage,
Give it a shine and luster.

The Vessel Glitters in the sun
As experience and learning
Pour through it.

At the end
Polished with wisdom
The goblet is mostly
Empty.

But even as you mourn
What's lost,
Your memories ignite it
To a luminous brightness.

Andrew Bienkowski

Tulips

Tulips still remind me of you.

Beauty and Intelligence held inside,
Ready to reveal to the world.

Blooming on your own terms,
Not following those around you.

Your bright vibrant flowers
Will remain with me forever.

Forgive me if I have taken
Them for granted.

Tim Bienkowski

4 WHO AM I

I Am

I am the product of my past.
I am the master of my future.
What I feel at this moment
Is the result of how I handled
The moments that just passed.
How I will feel tomorrow
Will be the result of how
I deal with the events today.

> The events of our lives,
> Yesterday, today and tomorrow
> Are only 10%
> Of the stories of our lives.
> The other 90%
> Are how we dealt
> With those events.

I am shaping my next life
With every decision,
Every choice,
Every action,
Every thought,
                    Today.

Andrew Bienkowski

Spiritual Side

More than just
Bodies, positions, deeds,
Ego, thoughts, emotions.

Our Soul ever present,
To know it's nature,
To grow, connect.

To spread light, healing,
To see us all as one,
To help each other,
And so ourselves.

To learn truths,
Love over fear,
Forgetting ego.
Move thoughts to words to change,
Appreciate others,
From our unique place.

Take a deep breath,
Clear your passages
To new ideas,
Search your soul,
You just might find
Yourself.

Tim Bienkowski

Meditation

Look inside,
With patience and focus,
You will find
A pool of calmness.

Go deeper yet
And find
Silence and peace.

At even deeper level
You will find
A glowing globe of love

At the very bottom
Of the deepest place
In your soul
You will discover wisdom.

And then my friend
You will realize
Who you really are:
A calm, silent, peaceful,
Loving and wise being,
Just looking at the world
Through your eyes.

Andrew Bienkowski

I Am

I am the blue moon that you see everyday.
A mystery vagrant in a street corner cardboard meadow.
Hope at the bottom of a sea of dust.
Dew drops of fear that cling to a dreamer's rainbow.
Candle wax dripping from tea light lovers' eyes

I am an open casket of sunflowers in crazy full bloom.
A gutless splinter in my own fingertip.
A brazen torpedo on a silky jet of water.
A seiche of sorrow that swells behind countless closed doors.

I am a tiny seed bursting with want.
A happy mystery trapped in a prison of understanding.
The truth in every denied subtlety.
The throwaway that gathers to a gorgeous collage.

I am a silly assumption in an unmade bed.
A genius with a tinker toy mind.
A lumbering feather drifting in place.
The petals of a clock whose chime fades with the wind.

I am the sweet chimney song of a starving winter sparrow.
An infinite explosion of butterflies expanding through the universe.
A fossil unfound through layers of time.
Everything that disappears and spins back upon itself.
I am a soft succulent rain shower shattering the spiny backbone of life.

Zoe Kothe

5 DREAMS

Awaken

Awareness clicks on like
A suddenly tuned radio.
The vivid landscape,
Crisp storyline,
And sweet sensations
Give way to
A soft pillow,
A familiar song,
And a sleepy body.

The woman of your dreams was just that.
The monsters of the night vanishing also.
Those determined moments of desire and emotion
Seem wasted as a ray of sunlight crosses your face.

The heaviness of your eyelids
And the gravity of your body
Become your momentary existence,
As the dust fills the sunbeams from above.

As you wiggle your toes,
And take a deep breath,
Remembering your waking role,
A voice inside tells you
Today's script is yours.
Fill it with your dreams.

Tim Bienkowski

Look, Listen and Touch

Look,
    In the mirror of your dreams
    My friend
    To know who you are.

Listen,
    To the echo of your words
    To grasp the meaning
    Of your soul.

Touch,
    The colors of the rainbow
    To feel the fingers of God.

And then,
    If you close your eyes,
    Will you know
    Where you are going.

Andrew Bienkowski

Dream

Dream my son,
When you close your eyes.

Dream of blue angels
With red bouquets,
Of floating over small towns
And open fields.

Dream of violins reverberating,
And soft kisses,
Sideways glances of knowing,
This is just a playful game.

Dream of listening to animals,
Who remind you of things,
That art is everywhere,
That love needs no name.

Dream of sailing down a lazy river,
Courageous toes hanging overboard.
A soft breeze coaxing you downriver,
No thoughts of turning back,
Your sails full with love.

Dream that all is well my son,
Dream that all
Is well.

Tim Bienkowski

6 SILENCE

Silence

It is difficult to let go
Of the world of sound.
We dread the emptiness of silences.
Perhaps because it reveals to us
The truths we do not want to hear.
We do not understand
That most words are not
An improvement on the absence of sound.
Silence can be frightening
If not approached properly.
It can be the cold silence
Of the arctic midnight stars.
Or the hot silence of the
Noontime desert sun.
At worst, it can be the screaming silence
Of a gun pointed at your head.
With reverence and a still mind
You will in the silence
Hear the eternal winds of time
And the background sound
Of the silent breath of God.
You don't choose this silence,
It chooses you.

Andrew Bienkowski

First Snow

A dreamlike silence blankets the waterfront.
The landscape's pearly white fresh paint
Growing thicker layer upon layer.

Soft wet snowflakes kiss our nose and cheeks,
As they twirl and float from the pale sky
Reluctantly falling to the earth.

We trudge on like five-year olds,
Punching paw shaped holes in the snow.
Following each other's tracks,
As if to confuse those who follow.

The sound of the crunching snow
And our muffled voices
Seem to diminish our impact in this place.
We are guests in an unfamiliar
Yet intimate new world.

Our bodies hidden in ghostlike coats,
We are but faces and voices,
Traversing hidden ground,
Glimpsing nature's simplest tapestry,
Watching our reflections in the snow.

Tim Bienkowski

Silence #2

The sound of silence
      echoes in my soul.

I listen, and I hear
      Ancient whispers,
Echoes of days gone by
When man and earth
And spirit were one.

      Whispers of the days to come
      When our souls will ring again
      In harmony with earth
      In the cosmic choir.

This silence flows
      Like a gentle river
In which I float
      and rest and dream.
It is in this silence
      that I trust,
And know
      who I am.

Andrew Bienkowski

7 WORDS

Words Need Releasing

Words need releasing.
Those among us know this.
But where are they hidden?
In a corner of our past,
On the horizon of our future,
Or on the tip of our consciousness?

Take some time to quiet yourself.
Undrape the towel around your body,
Lift the fogged-up glasses from your face.
Lay down near the window
Full of moonbeams and fill your paper with messages,
Origins unknown.

Tim Bienkowski

Words

Spoken words
Cut like a knife.

Puncture silence
Draining the peace
It contains.

Heal and create universes
Filled with beauty and joy.

Condense misty thoughts
Into concrete ideas.

Sometimes,
If there are too many,
Words create a fog,
That hides the truth
Within.

Spoken words
Have power
That creates
Good or evil.
So, be careful with words.

Andrew Bienkowski

Words

Words to live by.
I desire them.
Don't you?
The future scary in its vastness,
The past always there.
So many questions.
Give me the right words.

I want to tattoo them to my arms
Like a quarterback in a huddle with
The great philosophers.
What would they say?

Find joy in the faces that surround you.
Find beauty in the ordinary.
Breath deeply of the wind.
It is more than just air.

A wild bird flies by its own compass.
Needing no words.
Find your compass through silence.
Discover your destination
And fly there with grace.

Tim Bienkowski

Birth

It started as a seed-word,
  An idea,
    An awkward phrase.

It grew like a tumor
  Became big and heavy
Imprisoned inside
  Like a big bird
  A Thanksgiving turkey,
Demanding to be free.

You tire of carrying it.
Released painfully,
  It's a huge
    Disappointment.

What can you say
  Looking at your ugly
  Newborn baby-poem.
You can't
    Put it
      Back in.

Andrew Bienkowski

Hmmmm....

Maybe Bukowski was right.

It's a great relief when you release it.

It is best when not forced,
But freed in a natural way.

We cannot predict its rumblings,
Which prompt us when least expected.

We must be prepared for it
With paper nearby.

It is best accomplished in solitude
In a meditative state.

When it's completed we feel
A bit lighter on our feet.

Ah poetry....
I guess the same rules do apply.

Tim Bienkowski

A Poetry Reading

Poets gather

    For a "show and tell"

Showing each other

    Their soiled diapers

Shock value is measured

    In the odors, colors and texture

    Of the contents.

There is no beauty

    In this experience

There is nothing

    To be learned.

The pleasure lies

    In the wallowing.

Andrew Bienkowski

8 UNEARTHING

Postcards

Woman carries water from river to hut.

One small step for man....

Fences divide us into lesser parts.

Music adds curves to our perpendicular reality.

Not everyone likes oysters.

Maturity never fully arrives.

Cows outside their barn blush inwardly.

Still life is everywhere.

Examine with focus and magnification, but don't overstay the lens.

Would a tree second-guess its growth?

What do you think about black and white?

Knowledge is often best held from quivering lips.

Sadness can be quietly beautiful.

Ordinary things make up the extraordinary.

Green is the primary color of the earth.

Even the fallen can have their day.

Attention comes unexpectedly, have something to say.

Tim Bienkowski

Progress

You start with clear thinking,
Logic, making sense
Organizing, categorizing.

You go to understanding,
Wisdom, acceptance
Non-judgement.

You move to avoidance
of Wallowing
In the Past or Future
Expanding time
in the Now.

Then you start going
deeper, searching
for the stillness
of the mind, body and
Emotions.
Letting go of all attachments
of time and space
And dive into the
pool of Now
at the bottom of which
you find
Stillness.

Andrew Bienkowski

Proof

Flags are made of cloth,
But inspire blood.

Blood ties us together,
Revealing our frailties.

Fear is the bandage,
Blinding us from our wounds.

Wounds are self-inflicted,
But ones we must lick.

Lick a stamp, write that letter,
Seal the envelope.

Envelop your being with hope,
And drape it over you.

Like a flag,
On a clear, true day.

Tim Bienkowski

It's So Easy

It's so easy to be grateful for the good times in your life
For the love and friendship you receive
For the trees, stars, flowers, and colors in your life
For the good food and the full stomach.
For the beauty that you see and hear and touch.
For all the gifts that you have received from Mother Nature,
Other people, and God
It's so easy to be grateful.

It is so much harder to be grateful for
The suffering, pain, losses, mistakes, rejections.
And yet, and yet,
Those are the things we should be grateful for the most.
For they are the greatest source of learning, growth and wisdom.

Show me a man or woman who is very wise, and you can be sure
That they have had a great deal of pain and suffering in their lives.
That kind of gratitude you really have to work on. It is called
RADICAL GRATITUDE.

Andrew Bienkowski

Metaphors

My Lover is a Cherry Red Pine Tree, with fruit too dangerous to touch.

Your Darkness is a Tangerine Orange Bicycle, covered with mud.

A Belief is a Lime Green Stage, waiting for dress rehearsal.

A Teacher is an Ivory White Envelope, sealing your future with gold stars.

Tim Bienkowski

Diamonds

Blow away the dust
Wash the dirt away
Only diamonds will remain

Throw the lies away
Let go of the past
Only truth will remain

Let go of fear
Trust your heart
Only love will remain

Light the candle
Banish darkness
Only light will remain

With truth, love and light,
 In your heart
You will find
 Diamonds in your path

Andrew Bienkowski

9 TIME

Fast Life

Busy, busy, busy,
Don't waste time,
Hurry, multi-task.
Move faster and faster,
Yet we are always late,
Always behind
And cannot catch up.

The treadmill of life
is speeding up,
Going faster and faster
No time to stop
And smell the roses.

And yet, and yet,
At the end of this rush
Is a dead end.
You are dead.

Why such a hurry to get there?

The lucky ones discover,
That the speed of our life
Is not a movement
Toward something
But rather a flight
Away from something.

Running away from
Looking deeper
Into our souls
And running away
From real contacts
With each other.

So, to really live,
To taste real life,
Slow down,
Get off the treadmill,
And smell the roses.

Andrew Bienkowski

Heartbeat

We are but a heartbeat.
After all what better defines time
Than our ancient clock,
Telling us we are alive,
Counting off the moments.

Scientists have found that all animals
Have almost an identical number of heartbeats
Over the course of their lifetimes.

The cheetah is the James Dean
Of the animal kingdom,
Dancing quickly through life,
While the elephant plays the role of Orson Welles.
"There will be no wine before its time".

Why does our heart skip a beat
When we are in love, angry,
Or being chased by the lion.

Perhaps time is collapsing during our most intense moments,
Our heartbeat affecting the way we perceive time.

Meditation brings our heartbeat to a crawl,
Letting us almost erase time
And live only in our heart and soul.

Perhaps the heartbeat is like fuel.
The more we need from this earthly body,
The faster it needs to tick.

While everyone loves the excitement of a racing heart,
Perhaps we need to put our hearts to rest more,
And remember what it feels like
Before we had crimson muscles
To mark our time.

Tim Bienkowski

Time is a River

Time is a River
Flowing through the ages.

Safe in a boat,
Watch the world go by,
Uninvolved, detached,
Going where the river takes you.

Dive in and feel the cool wetness,
Swim and test the current.
Merge with the flow of time,
Testing the earthy sweetness of it.

Shooting the rapids
Full of danger and fear
Knowing that in time
Peaceful waters are not far.

Make peace with time,
Let the river carry you
Gently and softly
To the ocean called now,
Where all rivers meet
And become one.

Andrew Bienkowski

10 OUR DARKNESS

Night

Why do we fear darkness?
Is our vulgar fear of night
Only an echo
Of our caveman days?
Is it the fear of the unknown?

Then, let me tell you about night.

Long after sunset has died
And the advancing blackness
Has moved you away
From the violence of artificial light
Dark night reveals to you
The hidden face of nature
With its secrets and mysteries.

Approach this night with reverence,
Soak-in her silent poetry,
Listen to the dream like harmony
Of her seductive whispers.

She sings to you
In a silent captivating rhythm
Of the vastness of stars and space.
Let go of your fear
And if you are lucky
You will touch her holy and mystic face
In the dark.

Andrew Bienkowski

Fear

We live our lives like a $100 deductible
Collision policy with full replacement coverage.

We tell ourselves we are risk takers
As we play the stock market,
Act politically incorrect,
And have affairs at the office.

We forget about life and death,
Burning flesh and crumbling vertebrae,
Split second decisions,
Screaming in the dark for a loved one,
Carrying strangers beyond the flames.

Moments with no manuals to read,
No time for logic or reflection,
Just confusion and gut wrenching reactions.

We are forced to lose control,
And it is that which we most fear.
Control that makes us safe,
Chaos a step away from death.

So we bury this fear inside,
And when at last we cannot hide,
We feel that rush of terror
Move from stomach,
To chest to temple

Memories of childhood intensity
Revisit our psyche,
Wondering if we will indeed survive
The dog bite or
The belt buckle
Rattling behind us.

Tim Bienkowski

11 INJUSTICE

In The Name Of

In the name of
     Democracy
          Freedom
               Security

They are killed
     By the thousands
Civilians, children, old people.

We have done it well
     In Hiroshima, Nagasaki,
          Vietnam, Iraq.

It is all
     In the name of.

It's OK,
     We are still
          The good guys,

God is on our side

As we sing
     God Bless America

The killing goes on,

All in the name of.

Andrew Bienkowski

Justice?

Sand blowing, Tanks rolling,
Bombs glowing, Death-count growing,

Justice?

Political Games, Foolish claims,
Who-to-blames, Deadly flames,

Justice?

Payback a must, Vengeful lust,
Lives blown to dust, A nation crushed,

Justice?

A captured source, Judicial course,
Such deadly force, With no remorse,

Justice?

The decision clear, For all to hear,
But yet no fear, Though the end is here.

Justice?

Randy Bienkowski

The Killing

It would be a professional killing.
Word had come down from the top.
The time, place and circumstances had been decided on.
Orders given for an execution style killing.

He had left the organization a few years back
With some kills of his own,
And some differences of opinion.
But recent actions were indefensible,
It was his turn to die.

On June 11th, those in the organization
Followed their orders.
The papers would write about it.
The world watched.
Timothy McVeigh lay dead,
The organization went about its business.

Tim Bienkowski

12 FAMILY

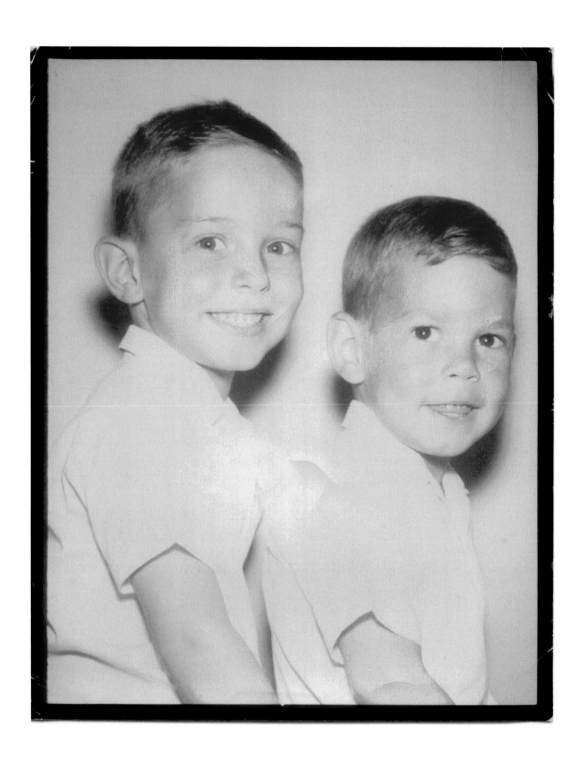

Brothers

We grew up in the same house,
Shared the same parents,
Many of the same thoughts.
But actions spoke differently,
Brothers who'd have thought.

We fought as kids,
You the physical one,
I the clever.

You the social,
I the introspective.

You the drummer,
I the brass player.

You the fearless,
I the follower.

You the spontaneous one,
I the digester.

I always saw you as my opposite.
It took awhile to understand,
Similarities were plentiful,
Just not choices made in hand.

Following in my footsteps,
Must not have been a breeze.
The leading edge was also hard,
Without a script to read.

The years strip by our differences,
That once seemed large in number.
The world treated us differently,
Let me help you my brother.

Tim Bienkowski

Grandma

I remember grandma…

Walking in the park on lazy afternoons,
Her round calloused hands holding mine,
Hard working hands with a hearty grip.

Her strong arms pushing me in circles
On my favorite merry-go-round,
Following my exclamations to go faster.

Her smiling gaze below me,
As I was king of the world
At the top of the slide.

Her flying next to me on a swing,
Never getting as high as I would,
But surpassing the FAA limits
For grandmothers.

I remember her buying me a strawberry cone
For the walk home,
Taking the long way,
So mom would never know.

I remember her tucking me in at night,
On that bed five feet off the floor.
A kiss on the cheek,
As she added another dime
To my metal bank,
My future surely secure.

Tim Bienkowski

13 AGING / LETTING GO

Tell Me When You Are Smiling

The world is fading
Into shadows.
Encroaching darkness
Bleeds the warmth
From my world.

What warms the heart
Is the touch of your hand,
The sound of your voice,
The love in your eyes,
Your beautiful smile.

In this world of shadows
I miss your smiling face
Shining with love, warmth,
Humor, interest and attention.

So when we talk
And I can't see your face,
Tell me
When you are smiling.

Andrew Bienkowski

Going Home

Frequent dreams remind me
That I do not belong.
Efforts to fit in
Become difficult and awkward
Due to difficulties
With vision, hearing, memory
And lack of energy.
In dreams I am always
Trying to find my way home.
Often lost,
Sometimes desperate.

Bonds with people we love
Keep us anchored to this world.
This earthly love is conditional.
What calls us to come home
Is the unconditional love
On the other side.

When you are born
Your friends on the other side
Feel sad about the difficult life
Ahead of you.
At the end of the journey
They are excited and welcome you back
It's a graduation party!
You are back from earth school.
What have you learned this time?

Andrew Bienkowski

Letting Go

The passage is easy
      if you let go.

Let go of fear, guilt, regret, worry,
                anxiety, concern.
Find a way to do it.
Replace it with love.

Let go of attachments to money,
      possessions, being right, ideology,
      past and future.
Replace it with living in the present.

As you gradually let go
      feel lighter (less heavy, less dark)
      feel more free (to choose)
      feel more peaceful
      feel closer to the other world.

You start realizing that
      all the things you hold on to
            hold you back,
                from moving on.
Effortlessly, easily, peacefully.

Andrew Bienkowski

The "Aaah" Experience

At the last moment
When all ceases to matter,
When body becomes heavy
And breathing is labored,

It is only if one
Remains calm and focused
That the passage
Is easy and painless.
There are flashes of wisdom
And glimpses of eternity
And it has been said
That it feels like
Removing tight uncomfortable shoes.
The "Aaah" experience.

Andrew Bienkowski

ABOUT THE AUTHORS

Tim Bienkowski currently works for the USPS and has been writing poetry since 2000 and taking photographs since the 1980's. He prefers nature photography and poetry of a personal nature. His previous book, <u>Postcards</u> was published in 2003, and he has had many poems published in the <u>Buffalo News</u>.

Andrew Bienkowski is a retired psychologist and has been writing poetry since around 2000 and prefers writing about philosophical subjects. He previously has published <u>Radical Gratitude (And Other Life Lessons Learned in Siberia)</u> with Mary Akers. This book has been published in seven countries in five languages. In the U.S. it has been published under the title <u>One Life To Give</u>.

Made in the USA
Monee, IL
09 October 2021